PARAGRAPH PRODUCTION

PARAGRAPH 1
TAKE 3

WRITTEN BY LINDA POLON
ILLUSTRATED BY BEV ARMSTRONG

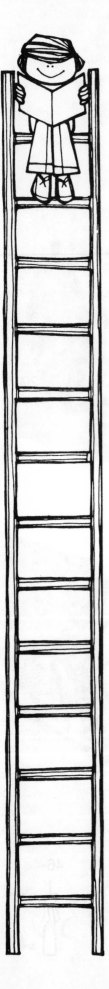

The Learning Works

THIS BOOK BELONGS

TO

_____

The purchase of this book entitles the individual teacher to
reproduce copies for use in the classroom.

Contents

To the Teacher

Paragraph Production consists of a series of activities designed to help students understand what paragraphs are and how to write and punctuate them correctly. These exercises are sequentially organized so that the more basic concepts are introduced and opportunities for related skill practice are provided before more complicated concepts are discussed.

On the first few pages, the author explains briefly what a paragraph is and then provides a series of exercises in which students are asked to read high-interest paragraphs and then to tell what each one is about and to select a title for it.

In the next group of exercises, the author explains that a story may contain more than one paragraph. Students are asked to read stories that are several paragraphs long and then to identify topic sentences and to match events with the story paragraphs in which they are described.

The author then points out the importance of staying on the topic, and the accompanying exercises involve choosing excluded sentences that might fit within a particular paragraph and identifying sentences that have been included but do not belong. Additional exercises cover ordering sentences logically, punctuating straight dialogue, and punctuating dialogue interspersed with narrative.

In the final group of exercises, students are presented with single situation pictures and then with picture sequences and are encouraged to use them as the bases for original paragraphs and multiparagraph stories.

Name _____

Choosing Seats and Losing Teeth

A **paragraph** tells about one idea or thing. A group of sentences that tells about one idea or thing is called a paragraph. Find out what the paragraphs below tell about.

1. Marty's trouble began on the first day of school. The teacher told class members that they could choose any seat they wanted but could not change seats later. Marty chose a seat near the window. He was happy until a girl sat down next to him.

   a. Underline the sentence that tells what this paragraph is about.
     (1) The seats in the classroom are near the window.
     (2) Marty likes school on the first day.
     (3) Marty's trouble at school began when he chose the wrong seat.

   b. Underline the best title for this paragraph.
     (1) Choosing Seats   (2) The Classroom   (3) Trouble for Marty

2. My baby brother was such a crybaby when his tooth was loose. I told him to be quiet, but he still cried. I opened the door and tied the tooth to the doorknob. Then I slammed the door shut. The tooth fell out. I smiled, but my brother still cried.

   a. This paragraph tells about (underline one)
     (1) brothers who do not get along.
     (2) using strings to yank out teeth.
     (3) a baby brother who cries because of a loose tooth.

   b. Underline the best title for this paragraph.
     (1) The Loose Tooth   (2) Playing Dentist   (3) How to Pull Teeth

Teeth Marks and Tetherballs

A **paragraph** tells about one idea or thing. A group of sentences that tell about one idea or thing is called a paragraph. Find out what the paragraphs below tell about.

1.   My math assignment was due in twenty minutes, and I couldn't find my pencil anywhere. Finally, I found it in my best friend's hand. When I asked him about it, he said it was his. I said it was mine, and he told me to prove it. I showed him my teeth and told him they matched the bite marks on the pencil. He must have believed me because he gave it back.

   a. This paragraph tells about (underline one)
      (1) a lost pencil found by its owner.
      (2) teeth marks on pencils.
      (3) math assignments that can't be done in twenty minutes.

   b. Underline the best title for this paragraph.
      (1) My Math Assignment
      (2) The Missing Pencil
      (3) Sharing Pencils

2.   One day I socked a tetherball really hard. Afterward, my hand hurt so much I thought I would die! In terrible pain, I rushed to the nurse's office, carefully holding my injured hand by the wrist. "I'll never play again," I thought. Suddenly, I saw a friend racing toward me. He told me the toughest kid in school had challenged me to a tetherball match. This was the chance I'd been waiting for! Then my friend saw my hand. He asked what was wrong. "Nothing," I said as I shook it vigorously. "Let's go back out to the school yard."

   a. This paragraph tells about (underline one)
      (1) school nurses.
      (2) an injured hand.
      (3) a tetherball match.

   b. Underline the best title for this paragraph.
      (1) The Great Tetherball Injury
      (2) Safety First
      (3) The School Nurse

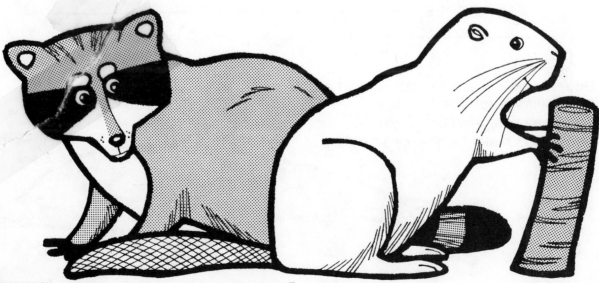

Raccoons and Beavers

A **paragraph** tells about one idea or thing. A group of sentences that tell about one idea or thing is called a paragraph. Find out what the paragraphs below tell about.

1.   The raccoon tiptoed down to the water's edge, a piece of food dangling from his small mouth. Carefully, he swirled the food in the cool stream. Then he lifted it and shook it rapidly. The food was now ready to eat.

    a. This paragraph tells about (underline one)
      (1) cool streams.
      (2) a raccoon who sits by the water to eat.
      (3) a raccoon who washes his food before he eats it.

    b. Underline the best title for this paragraph.
      (1) Cool Streams
      (2) Raccoon Food
      (3) Getting Ready to Eat

2.   A beaver popped his head out of the muddy river and tilted it to one side. Boom! A frightening noise echoed throughout the forest. The beaver shivered and ducked back into the water. He had to warn the other beavers of the danger. He raised his flat tail and slapped it loudly against the water's surface.

    a. Underline the sentence that tells what this paragraph is about.
      (1) Beavers live in streams.
      (2) Forest noises travel fast.
      (3) One beaver will warn other beavers of possible danger.

    b. Underline the best title for this paragraph.
      (1) The Frightening Noise
      (2) A Beaver's Day
      (3) The Beaver's Tail

Dolphins and Hyenas

A **paragraph** tells about one idea or thing. The first word in a paragraph is always indented. This means that it starts a little to the right of the left-hand margin. Rewrite the paragraphs below, indenting the first word. If you need more space, turn your paper over and continue on the back. Give each paragraph a title. Then answer the questions.

1. Dolphins can talk but not like humans. By blowing different amounts of air through their blowholes, they make squeaks, chirps, clicks, and whistles. They use these sounds to talk to other dolphins. When dolphins talk to one another, they make some sounds humans can't hear.

_____

_____

_____

_____

_____

_____

Underline the sentence that tells what this paragraph is about.
(1) Humans can talk better than dolphins.
(2) Dolphins can talk better than humans.
(3) Dolphins can talk by making sounds.

2. Hyenas are known as laughing animals. They don't laugh like human beings, though. When hyenas are nervous or are looking for food, they make laugh-like sounds. They make these sounds when they howl and gurgle at the same time.

_____

_____

_____

_____

_____

Underline the sentence that tells what this paragraph is about.
(1) Hyenas laugh like humans.
(2) Hyenas are always noisy.
(3) Hyenas make laugh-like sounds.

These Quills Are Not for Writing

A **paragraph** tells about one idea or thing. The first word in a paragraph is always indented. This means that it starts a little to the right of the left-hand margin. Rewrite the paragraph below, indenting the first word. If you need more space, turn your paper over and write on the back. Then answer the questions.

If a porcupine gets mad, it cannot shoot out its quills. The porcupine's quills are two to three feet long and razor sharp. Most of the time, they lie flat on the porcupine's body. When a porcupine becomes excited, it arches its back and the quills stand up. Then the porcupine swings its tail, trying to hit whatever is bothering it. Because the quills are not firmly attached, they come out easily when they brush against something.

_____

_____

_____

_____

_____

_____

_____

_____

a. **This paragraph tells** (underline one)
   (1) what porcupine quills look like and how they are used.
   (2) that porcupine quills make good pens.
   (3) that porcupines are mean animals.

b. **Underline the best title for this paragraph.**
   (1) The Dangerous Porcupine
   (2) Large Porcupines
   (3) Porcupine Quills

Wed.

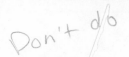

Don't d/o

The Pogo Stick Coincidence

A **story** can have more than one paragraph. Each new paragraph tells about a different idea or about things that happened at a different time. On another sheet of paper, copy the story written below. Don't forget to indent the first word of each paragraph. Then answer the questions.

1. Last Saturday morning, I went shopping with my mother to buy a holiday present for my best friend. My mother suggested that I buy a pogo stick. I laughed. "Those are for babies," I told her. "A kid my age wouldn't be seen on one!" Imagine a kid bobbing up and down like a yo-yo! Who would give a present like that? On second thought, though, it does look fun.

2. Later that afternoon, we were tired of looking, but I still couldn't decide what to buy. My mother reminded me about the pogo stick. I gave up and reluctantly agreed to her suggestion. We bought the pogo stick for my friend, and I wondered if I'd like to have one. "Nah," I thought. "I'd be called a bouncing baby when my friends saw me on it."

3. A week later, my friend and I exchanged our gifts. I hoped he wouldn't laugh. Instead, he jumped on the pogo stick and started hopping around like a frog. I sighed with relief and opened my present. Wow! It was a pogo stick, too. Just what I wanted! I guess pogo sticks aren't just for babies after all. "What a great gift!" I thought.

a. On the line following each sentence, write 1, 2, or 3 to indicate that the event named by that sentence occurs in the first, second, or third paragraph.

(1) The presents are exchanged. _____

(2) The mother suggests what her son should buy. _____

(3) They buy a pogo stick. _____

(4) You find out that the boy and his mother are shopping. _____

(5) The boy's friend likes the present. _____

(6) The boy can't decide what to buy. _____

(7) The boy decides a pogo stick isn't for babies after all. _____

(8) The boy makes up his mind about what to buy. _____

(9) The boy finds out what his friend has bought for him. _____

(10) The boy feels that a kid his age wouldn't want a pogo stick. _____

b. Underline the best title for this story.

(1) Shopping   (2) A Holiday Present for a Friend   (3) Baby Toys

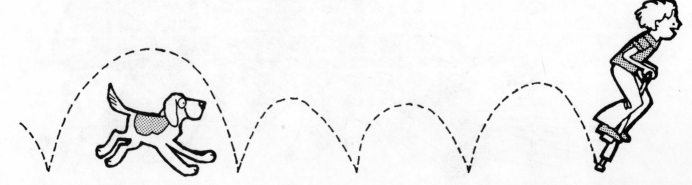

Who's Nervous Now?

A **story** can have more than one paragraph. Each new paragraph tells about a different idea or about things that happened at a different time. On a separate sheet of paper, copy the story written below. Don't forget to indent the first word of each paragraph. Then answer the questions.

1. The other day, mother told me that I could visit my grandfather in San Francisco. I asked if I could take the plane by myself. "I am a big girl, now," I told her. She replied that she knew I was growing up, but that flying alone was . . . I wouldn't let her finish. I pleaded. At last she agreed. I could see she was nervous, but I could hardly wait.

2. The day of the trip finally came. Mother fussed over me at the airport. She fiddled with my clothes and hair and kissed me two hundred zillion times. Then she asked if I'd packed my toothbrush and enough clean underwear. Her hand shook as she gave me a sack full of homemade chocolate chip cookies. I suggested we walk around the airport. I thought walking might calm her down.

3. Nearly an hour later, my flight was called and it was time to board the plane. Mother asked if I wanted her to come with me. Confidently, I told her I was going to be all right. I climbed the ramp and then turned and blew her a kiss before I walked on the plane. I took a seat and gazed out the window. As the plane took off, I felt my knees shaking. I wished my mother had come.

a. On the line following each sentence, write 1, 2, or 3 to indicate that the event named by that sentence occurs in the first, second, or third paragraph.
   (1) The girl's mother asks if she packed her toothbrush. _____
   (2) The girl begs to take the plane by herself. _____
   (3) The mother asks if the girl wants her to come along. _____
   (4) The girl feels her knees shaking. _____
   (5) The day of the trip finally comes. _____
   (6) The mother gives the girl a sack of cookies. _____
   (7) You first find out that the girl can hardly wait for the trip. _____
   (8) The mother fusses over her child. _____
   (9) The girl boards the airplane. _____
   (10) The girl wishes her mother had come with her. _____

b. Underline the best title for this story.
   (1) The Nervous Mother   (2) Eating on Planes   (3) Flying Alone

A Bone That Isn't Funny and a Rat That Doesn't Drink

Every paragraph has a **topic sentence**. The topic sentence tells the reader what the paragraph is about. It usually comes at the beginning of the paragraph. In each paragraph below, underline the topic sentence and then write it on the lines.

1. Hitting your funny bone is not really funny. When you hit your elbow in a certain spot, you get a painful, tingling feeling in your arm. This feeling sometimes goes all the way down into your fingers. When you hit your arm and get this feeling, people say you've hit your funny bone; but you haven't hit a bone at all. Instead, you've hit a nerve that lies near the surface of the skin. When it is struck, this nerve sends out pain messages.

    a. Write the topic sentence on the lines below.

    _____

    _____

    b. Underline the best title for this paragraph.
    (1) The Bones in Your Arm
    (2) The Nerves in Your Arm
    (3) Your Funny Bone

2. The kangaroo rat never drinks water. This small, rodent-like animal lives in the southwestern deserts of the United States where the weather is dry and little water is available. It gets the moisture it needs from the plants and roots that it eats.

    a. Write the topic sentence on the lines below.

    _____

    _____

    b. Underline the best title for this paragraph.
    (1) Desert Animals
    (2) Dry Land
    (3) The Kangaroo Rat

Weather Predictions, Wishes, and Dreams

Every paragraph has a **topic sentence**. The topic sentence tells the reader what the paragraph is about. Usually it comes at the beginning of the paragraph. For each paragraph below, underline the topic sentence and then write it on the lines.

1. The groundhog is supposed to be able to predict the weather. Each year on February 2, after sleeping all winter, this animal pops his head out of a hole in the ground. It is believed that, if the sun is shining and the groundhog sees his shadow, he will crawl back into his hole and sleep, and there will be six more weeks of winter. On the other hand, if the day is cloudy and the groundhog doesn't see his shadow, he will stay out of his hole, and spring will have officially arrived.

    a. Write the topic sentence on the lines below.

    _____

    _____

    b. Underline the best title for this paragraph.
    (1) Let Sleeping Groundhogs Lie
    (2) Fun in the Sun
    (3) How Groundhogs Predict the Weather

2. Most of your dreams are based on things that have happened to you in your life. They may have happened earlier that same day or a week, a month, or a year or more before. Your dreams may be happy, scary, sad, or funny. Sometimes they involve wishes that you want to come true or fears that you have.

    a. Write the topic sentence on the lines below.

    _____

    _____

    _____

    b. Underline the best title for this paragraph.
    (1) Dreams
    (2) Dreams and Fears
    (3) Dreams and Wishes

The Bears and the Bees

Every paragraph has a **topic sentence**. The topic sentence tells the reader what the paragraph is about. Usually it comes at the beginning of a paragraph, but sometimes it comes at the end. For each paragraph below, underline the topic sentence and then write it on the lines.

1.   Mammals are one type of animal that scientists classify. Other types of animals are fish, reptiles, birds, and amphibians.

   To be mammals, animals must share certain characteristics. All mammals have hair, are warm-blooded, give birth to live young, and breathe with lungs.

   Bats, bears, dogs, elephants, gerbils, giraffes, kangaroos, lions, whales, and zebras are mammals. Human beings are mammals, too. There are many different kinds of mammals.

Write the topic sentence for each paragraph on the lines below.

a. First paragraph _____

_____

b. Second paragraph _____

_____

c. Third paragraph _____

_____

2.   Forty to eighty thousand bees live together in a beehive. More than half of them are female worker bees. The rest are male bees known as drones. One queen bee rules the hive.

   All the bees in the hive have jobs. The queen lays eggs. The drones fertilize her so she can lay eggs. All the work in the hive is done by the female workers. They clean and guard the hive, take care of the young, and collect nectar to make honey.

Write the topic sentence for each paragraph on the lines below.

a. First paragraph _____

_____

b. Second paragraph _____

_____

Name _____

The Tallest and the First

Every paragraph has a **topic sentence**. The topic sentence tells the reader what the paragraph is about. Usually it comes at the beginning of the paragraph, but sometimes it comes at the end. For each paragraph below, underline the topic sentence and then write it on the lines.

1. Giraffes are the tallest animals in the world. They are so tall because they have long legs and necks.

    Giraffes are vegetarians. They find most of their food in trees. Because they are tall, it is easy for them to nibble the tender leaves that grow near the top.

    Giraffes like other giraffes. They also enjoy the company of other animals such as antelopes. Giraffes are gregarious.

Write the topic sentence for each paragraph on the lines below.

a. First paragraph _____

b. Second paragraph _____

c. Third paragraph _____

2. Someone cut in front of me in line. It happened yesterday when I lined up outside my classroom. I told the person to move, but he didn't. I decided to forget it.

    Before recess, as I lined up to go outside, someone else cut in front of me. I decided to forget it.

    At lunchtime, another person took cuts. I hollered to the teacher. She nodded and told the boy to go to the end of the line. He didn't. I decided to forget it, but I was angry.

    Today my problem was solved. We held classroom elections. I was elected line leader. Now **nobody** can step in front of me.

Write the topic sentence for each paragraph on the lines below.

a. First paragraph _____

b. Second paragraph _____

_____

c. Third paragraph _____

_____

d. Fourth paragraph _____

Thurs.

Puffers, Pandas, Tongues, and Horns

Remember that the topic sentence tells the reader what a paragraph is about. After each paragraph below, there are three topic sentences. Read each paragraph. Then select and underline the best topic sentence for that paragraph.

1. When this fish feels threatened, it makes itself larger. It puffs itself up with air or water. The puffer's body becomes as hard as a football.

    a. The puffer is a saltwater fish.

    b. The puffer lives in the warmest part of the ocean.

    c. The puffer has a simple way of protecting itself.

2. These jungles are located on mountains. Because the panda feeds on bamboo, he stays close to home.

    a. The panda lives a quiet life.

    b. The panda lives in bamboo jungles.

    c. The panda belongs to the raccoon family.

3. They do not do so because they are preparing to strike. Snakes use their tongues to feel, touch, and pick up food.

    a. Snakes swallow their food whole.

    b. Snakes come in all sizes.

    c. Snakes slither along flicking their tongues in and out.

4. It is made up of a bunch of matted hairs. These hairs form a long point on the rhino's head. This horn keeps growing throughout the rhino's life. To keep the horn from getting too long, the rhino rubs it against a tree or stone.

    a. A rhino's horn is not a real horn.

    b. African natives hunt the rhino for its horn.

    c. Rhinos that live in zoos grow shorter horns than those that roam the African plains.

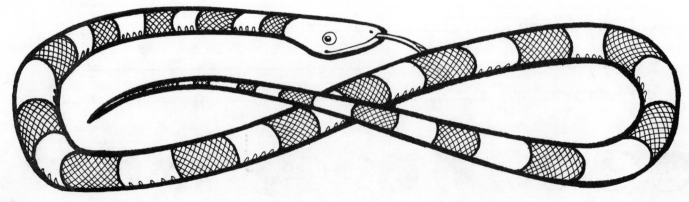

Trunks, Suits, Pouches, and Spines

Remember that a topic sentence tells the reader what a paragraph is about. After each paragraph below, there are three topic sentences. Read each paragraph. Then select and underline the best topic sentence for that paragraph.

1. Some of these uses are smelling, drinking, and feeding. The elephant never swallows with its trunk. It uses its trunk to suck in food and water. Then it places the food and water in its mouth.

    a. The elephant has a long trunk.

    b. Near an elephant's trunk are tusks.

    c. An elephant's trunk has many uses.

2. It wears a coat of thick, heavy fur. It even has hair between its toes.

    a. The polar bear is well suited to live in the snow.

    b. The polar bear is an excellent swimmer because of its fur.

    c. A polar bear's fur is not waterproof.

3. After the female lays the eggs, the male carries them in a pouch on his stomach. The eggs develop in the pouch for five weeks. Then the little seahorses swim out.

    a. Most seahorses are only one or two inches long.

    b. The strangest thing about a seahorse is the way it raises its young.

    c. A seahorse lays eggs in the ocean.

4. Its body is covered with sharp spines. When it is frightened or feels in danger, it rolls itself into a ball. Special muscles allow the hedgehog to do this.

    a. The hedgehog has a unique way of protecting itself.

    b. The hedgehog is a small animal.

    c. The hedgehog does not live in America.

Name _____

Underground, Underwater, or in a Tree

Remember that a topic sentence tells the reader what a paragraph is about. After each paragraph below, there are three topic sentences. Read each paragraph. Then select and underline the best topic sentence for that paragraph.

1. It is built to tunnel through the earth. It has a pointed nose and a strong body. It uses its body and nose for pushing dirt and its sharp claws for digging.

   a. A mole likes to eat earthworms.

   b. A mole lives underground.

   c. The mole is well suited for living underground.

2. The mother hippo feeds its baby milk underwater. Although the baby eats underwater, it cannot breathe underwater. It must rise to the surface at times for air.

   a. A baby hippo is born underwater.

   b. A baby hippo looks like its parents in the water.

   c. A baby hippo can swim well.

3. An elephant's skin is tender. Under a one-inch-thick skin, though, there is a layer of fat. This fat insulates the elephant and keeps it warm or cool.

   a. An elephant's skin can wrinkle in the cold.

   b. An elephant looks like it has enough skin to keep it warm or cool, but it doesn't.

   c. An elephant's skin is gray.

4. Only once in a while does it come down to the ground. It comes down from one tree to move to another tree or to lick the ground. Licking the ground somehow helps the koala digest its food.

   a. The koala likes looking at the ground.

   b. The koala stays in trees most of the time.

   c. The koala eats a lot of leaves.

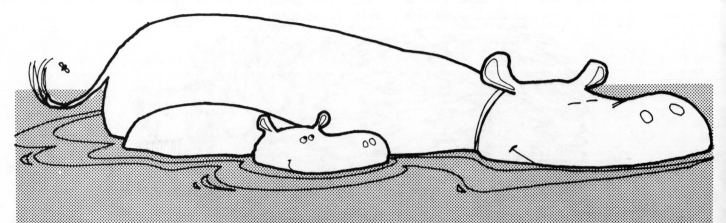

Yo-Yos

A paragraph tells about one idea or thing. There are three paragraphs in this story, but it is written as one. Look for the different topics. Circle the first word in each paragraph. Then write the topic sentence of each paragraph on the lines below and underline the best title for this story. On the back of this sheet or on a separate piece of paper, write the story in correct paragraph form. Don't forget to indent the first word of each new paragraph.

Where did the yo-yo come from? Pictures of yo-yos appear on vases that were made during the eighth century in Greece. We don't know how the Greeks used them. Yo-yos were used as weapons in the Philippines several hundred years ago. These yo-yos were stones attached to long strings. Hunters sat in trees and waited for animals to come by. As the animals passed below, the hunters dropped the stones on their heads. If people were involved in fights, they hurled the stones at their enemies. Yo-yos were useful as weapons because they would come back to the thrower and could be thrown over and over again. It wasn't until 1920 that yo-yos became popular in the United States. In that year, the Duncan Toy Company sold millions of them. Children liked yo-yos because they could do tricks with them.

1. **Write the topic sentence for each paragraph on the lines below.**

   a. First paragraph _____

   _____

   b. Second paragraph _____

   _____

   c. Third paragraph _____

   _____

2. **Underline the best title for this story.**

   a. Yo-Yo Tricks
   b. Yo-Yos As Weapons
   c. The History of the Yo-Yo

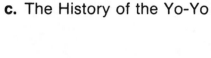

Old Four Eyes

A paragraph tells about one idea or thing. There are four paragraphs in this story, but it is written as one. Look for the different topics. Circle the first word in each paragraph. Then write the topic sentence of each paragraph on the lines below and underline the best title for this story. On the back of this sheet or on a separate piece of paper, write the story in correct paragraph form. Don't forget to indent the first word of each new paragraph.

One Saturday afternoon when I went to the eye doctor, he told me I needed glasses. "What could be worse?" I thought. I just knew my school friends would tease me. I could hear them calling me "old four eyes." Several weeks later, I got my glasses. My mother told me I had to wear them to school. On the next day, I made sure to keep them in my shirt pocket. When my friend asked about the bulge in my pocket, I wouldn't tell him what it was. Later in the day, I was called on to read. I blinked my eyes, but the words were fuzzy. I knew it was time, so I slowly pulled out my glasses and slid them on. I slouched in my chair and didn't dare look up. I knew everyone was staring at me as I read. Just as I finished, I felt a tap on my shoulder. It was my friend. He was smiling at me. I sat up in my seat and smiled back when I saw that he was wearing new glasses, too.

1. **Write the topic sentence for each paragraph on the lines below.**

   a. First paragraph _____

   _____

   b. Second paragraph _____

   _____

   c. Third paragraph _____

   _____

   d. Fourth paragraph _____

   _____

2. **Underline the best title for this story.**

   a. New Glasses
   b. Teasing Friends
   c. Reading Well with New Glasses

South American Sleeper

A paragraph tells about one idea or thing. There are four paragraphs in this story, but it is written as one. Look for the different topics. Circle the first word in each paragraph. Then write the topic sentence of each paragraph on the lines below and underline the best title for this story. On the back of this sheet or on a separate piece of paper, write the story in correct paragraph form. Don't forget to indent the first word of each new paragraph.

A sloth is a strange-looking animal from South America. It weighs about ten pounds and is about as long as a small to medium-sized dog. Its head is shaped like a monkey's. When it hangs upside down, the sloth looks like a brown, shaggy dog covered with long, strawlike fur. When it lies on the ground, it looks like a shaggy doormat. Many people consider the sloth to be a lazy animal because it spends most of its time in trees and moves slowly. Actually, the sloth is nearly helpless on the ground. It can only drag itself along because its legs aren't strong enough to hold it up. Scientists feel that one reason the sloth moves slowly is because it has a low body temperature. The sloth sleeps a lot. It sleeps from fifteen to eighteen hours a day without moving. When a sloth is sleeping, it hangs upside down from a tree branch. When a sloth isn't sleeping, it is eating. It reaches out with its long arm and grabs leaves and juicy fruit. Sometimes a sloth won't eat because it can't make up its mind what it wants. Once it starts, though, it really eats.

1. **Write the topic sentence for each paragraph on the lines below.**

   a. First paragraph _____

   _____

   b. Second paragraph _____

   _____

   c. Third paragraph _____

   _____

   d. Fourth paragraph _____

   _____

2. **Underline the best title for this story.**

   a. Monkey Face
   b. The Sloth
   c. Sleepy Animal

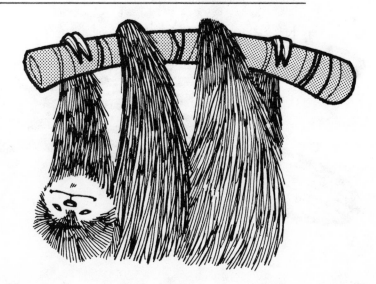

One Million Eggs!

A paragraph tells about one idea or thing. Some ideas or things belong in a paragraph and others do not. Below is a paragraph and a group of sentences. Read the paragraph carefully. Then choose and write the sentences that could fit into the paragraph. On a separate sheet of paper, rewrite the paragraph, inserting the sentences you have chosen.

The female goldfish has a lot of children. Each year she lays between 500,000 and 1,000,000 eggs. These eggs usually stick to water plants. It takes between five and nine days for the eggs to hatch. After they hatch, the small goldfish remain near the plants for a couple of days. Then, they swim away.

Which of these sentences could fit into the paragraph above?

1. A goldfish lays her eggs between May and August.
2. In the wild, beetles are the enemies of goldfish.
3. When the water is warm, the eggs hatch quicker.
4. When a goldfish is eighteen days old, it is almost one inch long.

Write the sentences that fit on the lines below.

_____

_____

_____

_____

_____

_____

_____

_____

An Animal That Stinks

A paragraph tells about one idea or thing. Some ideas or things belong in a paragraph and others do not. Below is a paragraph and a group of sentences. Read the paragraph carefully. Then choose and write the sentences that could fit into the paragraph. On a separate sheet of paper, rewrite the paragraph, inserting the sentences you have chosen.

A skunk has an interesting way of protecting itself when it feels threatened. At first it stamps its feet. Next, it shoots up its tail. Like a cat, the skunk arches its back. Then the skunk squirts a stream of smelly liquid at its enemy. The skunk can do this while standing with its back to its enemy or while facing its enemy. All it does is bend its body a little.

Which of these sentences could fit into the paragraph above?

1. The skunk also makes chattering sounds when it is frightened.
2. The smelly liquid can travel up to twelve feet.
3. Skunks can swim but not climb.
4. When a skunk shoots out the liquid five or six times, it uses up the supply and must wait a few days for its body to make more.
5. The horned owl likes to hunt skunks.

Write the sentences that fit on the lines below.

_____

_____

_____

_____

_____

_____

_____

How Paper Is Made

A paragraph tells about one idea or thing. Some ideas or things belong in a paragraph and others do not. Below is a paragraph and a group of sentences. Read the paragraph carefully. Then choose the sentences that could fit into the paragraph. On a separate sheet of paper, rewrite the paragraph, inserting the sentences you have chosen.

Most of the paper you write on is made from wood. Trees are cut and sent to a paper mill where they are shredded into chips. These chips are boiled and mixed with chemicals to turn them into a soggy, mushy pulp. The pulp is washed and bleached, and a type of chalk is added to make the paper white. Then the mixture is placed in a machine with a screen. The water in the pulp drains out through the screen. The remaining pulp is pressed and rolled several times and turned into long sheets of paper.

Which of these sentences could fit into the paragraph above?

1. Paper is also made from rags, rope, wastepaper, and straw.
2. There are many forests loaded with Christmas trees.
3. After the pulp has been washed and bleached and the chalk has been added to it, it is called "stuff."
4. Wallpaper comes in all colors.
5. To make writing paper, cotton and rag fibers are added to the pulp as it is being rolled.

Write the sentences that fit on the lines below.

_____

_____

_____

_____

_____

_____

_____

Cactus, Crickets, and Squid

A paragraph tells about one idea or thing. Every paragraph has a topic sentence. This sentence tells the reader what the paragraph is about. All of the other sentences in the paragraph must tell about the idea or thing named or described in the topic sentence. This is called **staying on the topic**.

In each paragraph below, one sentence does not belong. Underline the sentence that does *not* belong. Then write it on the lines below the paragraph.

1.   It's time to go home, and the teacher won't even notice me. I'm sitting up straight and tall. I love to slouch in my chair at home when I'm watching television. My desk is neat, but she's letting everybody else go first. When will she look my way?

_____

_____

2.   A cactus plant gets very little water because it grows in the desert where there is not much rain. A lot of people keep cactus plants in their homes. When it does rain, the cactus roots take in a great deal of water. This water is then stored in the plant's stem.

_____

_____

3.   Only the male cricket makes music. It chirps to get the attention of the female. For years, the Japanese kept crickets in cages as pets. Under each of the cricket's wings is a rough surface and a scraper. When the cricket rubs its two wings together, the scraper rubs the rough surface to make the music.

_____

_____

4.   The squid has an interesting way of escaping from its enemies. When it feels threatened, it squirts out a dark liquid. This liquid clouds the water and makes it hard for an enemy to see the squid. The squid is related to the octopus. The squid then swims quickly away.

_____

_____

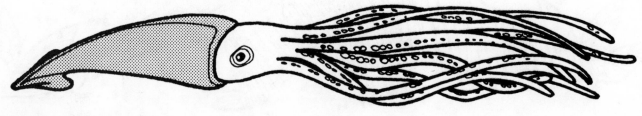

The Llama, the Anteater, and the Pelican

A paragraph tells about one idea or thing. Every paragraph has a topic sentence. This sentence tells the reader what the paragraph is about. All of the sentences in a paragraph must tell about the idea or thing named or described in the topic sentence. This is called **staying on the topic.**

In each paragraph below, one sentence does not belong. Underline the sentence that does *not* belong. Then write it on the lines below the paragraph.

1. The llama has an interesting way of defending itself when it is frightened or bothered. Incidentally, the llama comes from South America. The llama grits its teeth and spits a bad-smelling liquid at its enemy. Usually, the llama is an extremely accurate spitter.

_____

_____

2. The great anteater is about the size of a small bear. It has long, brown fur and a bushy tail. At the tip of its very long, pointed head, it has an unusually small mouth with no teeth. The anteater catches ants with its long, sticky tongue. I think it would be great to have an anteater at a picnic!

_____

_____

3. Things weigh less on the moon. Because the moon is smaller than the earth, the pull of gravity is less on the moon. On the moon, objects weigh only one-sixth of what they would weigh on earth. People started traveling to the moon many years ago. For example, a person who weighs 84 pounds on earth would weigh 14 pounds on the moon.

_____

_____

4. A pelican's mouth is perfect for fishing. If you go to the beach, you can see a pelican. When a pelican spots a school of fish, it opens its mouth and scoops the fish into its pouch. Then it shuts its mouth and the water drains out. The pelican's pouch can stretch to hold up to thirty one-pound fish.

_____

_____

Name _____

Playing 'Possum

A paragraph tells about one idea or thing. Every paragraph has a topic sentence. This sentence tells the reader what the paragraph is about. All of the sentences in a paragraph must tell about the idea or thing named or described in the topic sentence. This is called **staying on the topic.**

In each paragraph below, one or more of the sentences do not belong. Underline the sentences that do *not* belong. Then write them on the lines below the paragraph.

1.   Did you know that an **octopus** can change its color? One minute it can be red, brown, or purple, and the next minute it can turn blue, **gray,** or white. Inside the octopus's skin are pigment bags. An octopus has eight **legs.** These bags are filled with coloring matter. The bags are connected to the octopus's nervous system. An octopus can grow another leg if it loses one. When the octopus becomes frightened, nervous, or excited, these bags release the coloring matter and the octopus turns a different color.

_____

_____

_____

2.   Spiders don't get caught in their own webs. They spin them of two types of thread. One is sticky, and the other is not. Not all spiders are poisonous. To move about their webs, spiders walk on the nonsticky threads.

_____

_____

_____

3.   An opossum has a special way of protecting itself. When it feels threatened, it faints. The female opossum has a pouch on her stomach. She carries her newborn babies in this pouch. The opossum falls to the ground, closes its eye, and plays dead. Most animals are deceived by the opossum's trick. They go away and leave this clever animal alone.

_____

_____

Name _____

Beavers, Bees, and Otters

A group of sentences that tell about one thing is called a paragraph. A paragraph is easier to understand if the sentences it contains are in logical order.

The sentences in each paragraph below are not in correct order. On a separate sheet of paper, rewrite each paragraph so that the sentences it contains are in correct order.

1.   Once built, the dam slows down the flow of the river so that the beavers have quiet waters in which to live. They carry the tree branches and twigs to the river and place them on the bottom. To build a dam, beavers must chop down trees. They combine rocks and mud with the branches and twigs to build a dam.

2.   The house bees add a chemical from their bodies to the nectar. Honeybee workers gather flower nectar for their hives. The bees fill the honeycomb cells in their hives with this honey and seal the cells with wax. As water evaporates from the nectar, it is turned into honey. They keep the nectar in their stomachs until they give it to the house bees.

3.   He pounds the crab or lobster with the rock. Then, he swims to the ocean bottom looking for a rock. When the shell cracks, the otter eats the meat from the shell while still floating on his back. A sea otter likes to eat shellfish, but he has a different way of getting the meat out of the shell. First he finds a crab or lobster. After he finds a rock, he swims to the surface and rolls over on his back.

Hit and Run

A group of sentences that tell about one thing is called a paragraph. A paragraph is easier to understand if the sentences it contains are in logical order.

The sentences in each paragraph below are not in correct order. On a separate sheet of paper, rewrite each paragraph so that the sentences it contains are in correct order.

1.   The shortstop relayed the ball to the catcher at home plate. She sprinted easily to first base, then on to second. The girl slid into home just ahead of it. The batter socked the ball into the outfield. She was safe and had scored a run. As an outfielder bobbled the ball, she flew by third and headed home. At last, the outfielder scooped up the elusive ball and threw it to the shortstop.

2.   She opened her umbrella and marched outside. From the window, the girl saw that it was raining. The rain stopped. Resignedly, she put on her raincoat, hat, and boots.

3.   I don't like to put my paper on the top of the pile, so I carefully placed it near the bottom. Then I watched as everyone else did the same thing. When the spelling test was over, I put my paper on the teacher's desk. I can't win!

4.   I had to dance with a girl. At least, I'm still alive! I just knew I was going to get cooties, itch all over, and maybe die. We had a holiday dance at school. But I tried it, and it wasn't so bad after all.

Shrews and Kangaroos

Sentences in a paragraph contain information about the topic of the paragraph. Below are two paragraphs. Read these paragraphs and then decide what questions are answered by the information in each. Write these questions on the lines provided. The first question relating to each paragraph has been written for you.

1. The kangaroo has a useful tail. Because of its tail, this animal can jump twenty feet or more. The kangaroo's tail helps stabilize it in the air as it leaps. When the kangaroo lands on the ground, its tail helps support it. The kangaroo also uses its tail for support while sitting. When the kangaroo is tired, it leans back and rests its weight against its tail.

    a. What is the topic sentence of this paragraph? _____

    _____

    b. What questions about kangaroos does this paragraph answer?

    (1) How far can a kangaroo jump?

    (2) _____

    (3) _____

    (4) _____

    c. Write one additional sentence that would fit into this paragraph.

    _____

2. The shrew is one of the hungriest animals in the world. It is also one of the smallest. The shrew is so small that it could easily fit into a pocket. It spends all of its waking hours eating. It lives on juicy, delicious worms and insects. Many times a day, the shrew eats an amount of food equal to its weight. Because it eats all the time, looking for food is a full-time job for the shrew.

    a. What is the topic sentence of this paragraph? _____

    _____

    b. What questions about shrews does this paragraph answer?

    (1) What is the name of one of the hungriest animals in the world?

    (2) _____

    (3) _____

    (4) _____

    c. Write one additional sentence that would fit into this paragraph.

    _____

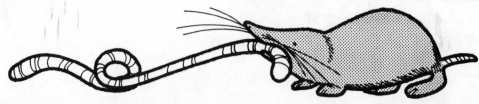

A Six-Legged Treat

Sentences in a paragraph contain information about the topic of the paragraph. Below is a paragraph. Read this paragraph and then decide what questions can be answered with the information in the paragraph. Write these questions on the lines provided.

Some black honey ants from South America are always filled with food. These ants are stuffed like teddy bears with honey by other worker ants. When there is plenty of food, their full stomachs swell to the size of a grape. When food becomes scarce, the stuffed ants throw up the sweet-smelling honey. Then the other ants in the colony have plenty of food to eat. People who live in South America sometimes eat the stomachs of honey ants as a treat similar to candy.

1. **What is the topic sentence of this paragraph?**

   _____

   _____

2. **What questions about black honey ants does this paragraph answer?**

   a. _____

   b. _____

   c. _____

   d. _____

   e. _____

3. **Write one additional sentence that would fit into this paragraph.**

   _____

   _____

Lost and Found

A **dialogue** is a written conversation between two or more persons. When a different speaker begins speaking in a dialogue, a new paragraph must be started.

Rewrite the following dialogue on another sheet of paper. Remember to start a new paragraph each time a different speaker begins speaking and to indent the first word of each new paragraph. The paragraphs below are numbered so that you can easily see where a new one should begin.

1. "I lost my sweater, and my mother will kill me if I don't find it," Sandy wailed to her best friend, Marla.

2. "Where do you think you lost it?" asked Marla.

3. "I wish I knew! I've looked everywhere I can think of—on the handball courts, in the classroom, in the cafeteria—and it's just no use. I can't find it anywhere," cried Sandy.

4. "Don't worry," said Marla, patting her friend reassuringly on the shoulder. "It's bound to show up."

5. "I wish I were as certain as you are," moaned Sandy. "It's brand new, and my mother will kill me if I go home without it."

6. "Have you looked in the Lost and Found?" asked Marla.

7. "Not yet," said Sandy as she started walking toward the office. Marla followed close behind.

8. "What color was your sweater?" asked Marla as they walked.

9. "Light blue," answered Sandy. "Light blue with white buttons. My grandmother made it for me."

10. "Is this it?" asked Marla, taking a light blue sweater from the Lost and Found box and holding it up for Sandy to see.

11. "Yes, that's it!" exclaimed Sandy. "Now mother won't kill me—at least, not for losing my sweater."

Out of Season but Okay

A **dialogue** is a written conversation between two or more persons. In written conversation, when a different speaker begins speaking, a new paragraph must be started.

Rewrite the following dialogue on another sheet of paper. Remember to start a new paragraph each time a different speaker begins and to indent the first word of each new paragraph.

"I hope the teacher doesn't read that note!" Maria exclaimed to her friend, George. "If she does, I'll be embarassed," answered George, blushing. "How *could* you have let her get it? You should have passed it under the table," said Maria, shaking her head in dismay. "I did. But how was I to know she was looking right at me when I did it?" responded George. "I wish I could crawl inside my desk and just hide there forever and ever and never have to come out and see you and Miss Brown again!" exclaimed Maria. "*You* wish *you* could hide," answered George. "*I'm* the one who wrote the note. And she's coming this way." "How sweet of you, George," said Miss Brown, as she approached his desk. "It's a little early for Valentine's Day, but thank you for the thought, even if it is a little out of season," continued Miss Brown as she walked on past George's desk smiling. George took a deep breath. "She thought the note was for her," he said. "I think I forgot to put your name on it, Maria." "Thank goodness you did," said Maria, taking a deep breath, too.

Bubble Trouble

Dialogue is the part of a story spoken by the characters. **Narrative** is the part of a story told by the author. When you mix dialogue with narrative, you must start a new paragraph each time you switch from one to the other. The only time the two may be kept in the same paragraph is when the narrative is about the speaker or what he or she is doing. For example,

> Marty handed Linda the present and said, "I hope you like it."
> He sat down on a chair, crossed his fingers, and nervously waited
> to see the look on her face. He really wanted Linda to be happy.

As you read the story below, mark the places where new paragraphs should begin. When you have finished reading and marking, rewrite the story on a separate sheet of paper. Remember to indent the first word of each new paragraph.

Tom and Steve sat in the back of the classroom listening to a math lesson and talking. "Will you *please* give me a piece of gum?" Steve asked Tom. "I only have one piece left. You'll get me in trouble," answered Tom, cautiously. Mrs. Butterfield wrote another problem on the board and then called on Tara to work it. "How can *I* get *you* into trouble? The teacher hasn't called on me all morning. She hasn't even looked this way," snapped Steve impatiently. "It's almost time for lunch. I'd wait if I were you," responded Tom. Steve blew on his fist and rubbed it against his chest. "You know I'm an expert chewer," he bragged. "I used to blow the biggest bubbles in class without ever being spotted. Why, one time I even chewed four pieces at once and didn't get caught." Tom laughed quietly. He put his hand over his mouth and said, "Yeah. I remember that time. The teacher thought you had mumps and called the school nurse to check the whole class. Boy, did you swallow that gum fast!" Steve shook his head and said, "Well, that was only once." As the boys continued to talk, Mrs. Butterfield told everyone to look at the problems she had written on the board. "These look easy," said Steve. He turned to Tom. "Can I have the gum now?" Reluctantly, Tom nodded and handed Steve a piece of gum. "This gum is great!" exclaimed Steve, chewing it briskly. Just as he blew the first bubble, Mrs. Butterfield called his name. "Steve," she said, pointing to the board, "can you give us the answer to that first problem?" Steve ducked behind his open math book, trying to hide the enormous bubble that covered the lower half of his face. Suddenly, Tom yanked Steve's shirt. The gum Steve had been hastily gathering back into his mouth flew straight toward Mrs. Butterfield. She slowly scraped the pink mass off her glasses and asked, "Where did *this* come from?" She glared at Steve. There was no answer from anyone. "All right, boys and girls, let's get back to work," she said in her most businesslike tone. Steve felt his heart beating like the kernels in a popcorn machine. He wiped his forehead and sighed, "That was a close one." "Guess what," said Tom. This is really your lucky day! I found another piece of gum in my pocket. For a moment, Steve stared at Tom in disbelief, then he began to work on his math assignment.

Name _____

Popper Power

Write a one-paragraph story describing this picture. Start with a topic sentence that tells what the paragraph is going to be about. Remember to indent the first word in the paragraph and to arrange the sentences in logical order. When you have finished writing, give your story a title.

_____

_____
_____
_____
_____
_____
_____
_____
_____
_____
_____
_____

Wishful Blowing

Write a one-paragraph story describing this picture. Start with a topic sentence that tells what the paragraph is going to be about. Remember to indent the first word in the paragraph and to arrange the sentences in logical order. When you have finished writing, give your story a title.

_____

_____

_____

_____

_____

_____

_____

_____

_____

_____

Batter Up!

Write a one-paragraph story describing this picture. Start with a topic sentence that tells what the paragraph is going to be about. Remember to indent the first word in the paragraph and to arrange the sentences in logical order. When you have finished writing, give your story a title.

_____

_____

_____

_____

_____

_____

_____

_____

_____

_____

_____

_____

The Screen Scene

Write a one-paragraph story describing this picture. Start with a topic sentence that tells what the paragraph is going to be about. Remember to indent the first word in the paragraph and to arrange the sentences in logical order. When you have finished writing, give your story a title.

_____

_____

_____

_____

_____

_____

_____

_____

_____

_____

_____

_____

_____

A Fine Specimen!

Write a one-paragraph story describing this picture. Start with a topic sentence that tells what the paragraph is going to be about. Remember to indent the first word in the paragraph and to arrange the sentences in logical order. When you have finished writing, give your story a title.

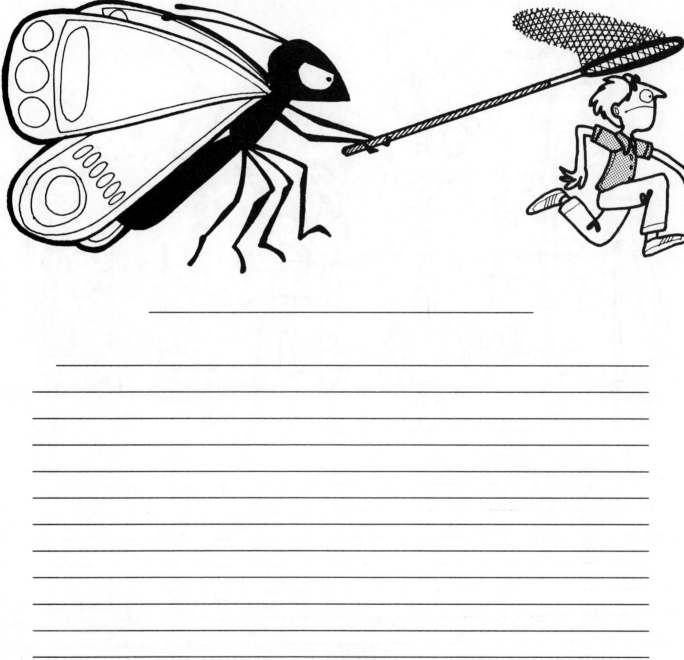

_____

_____
_____
_____
_____
_____
_____
_____
_____
_____
_____

Just What I Always Wanted!

Write a two-paragraph story about these pictures. Start each paragraph with a topic sentence that tells what the paragraph is going to be about. Remember to indent the first word in each paragraph and to arrange the sentences in logical order. If you need more space in which to write, continue on the back of this sheet or on a separate piece of paper. When you have finished writing, give your story a title.

_____

_____

_____

_____

_____

_____

_____

_____

_____

_____

I Love a Parade

Write a two-paragraph story about these pictures. Start each paragraph with a topic sentence that tells what the paragraph is going to be about. Remember to indent the first word in each paragraph and to arrange the sentences in logical order. If you need more space in which to write, continue on the back of this sheet or on a separate piece of paper. When you have finished writing, give your story a title.

_____

_____

_____

_____

_____

_____

_____

_____

_____

_____

_____

Name _____

Fancy Meeting *You* Here!

Write a two-paragraph story about these pictures. Start each paragraph with a topic sentence that tells what the paragraph is going to be about. Remember to indent the first word in each paragraph and to arrange the sentences in logical order. If you need more space in which to write, continue on the back of this sheet or on a separate piece of paper. When you have finished writing, give your story a title.

_____

Man Overboard!

Write a two-paragraph story about these pictures. Start each paragraph with a topic sentence that tells what the paragraph is going to be about. Remember to indent the first word in each paragraph and to arrange the sentences in logical order. If you need more space in which to write, continue on the back of this sheet or on a separate piece of paper. When you have finished writing, give your story a title.

_____

_____

_____

_____

_____

_____

_____

_____

_____

_____

_____

Name _____

The Care and Feeding of House Plants

Write a three-paragraph story about these pictures. Start each paragraph with a topic sentence that tells what the paragraph is about. Remember to indent the first word in each paragraph and to arrange the sentences in logical order. If you need more space in which to write, continue on the back of this sheet or on a separate piece of paper. When you have finished writing, give your story a title.

_____

_____

_____

_____

_____

_____

_____

_____

_____

_____

_____

A Horrifying Halloween Visit to Planet Earth

Write a three-paragraph story about these pictures. Start each paragraph with a topic sentence that tells what the paragraph is about. Remember to indent the first word in each paragraph and to arrange the sentences in logical order. If you need more space in which to write, continue on the back of this sheet or on a separate piece of paper. When you have finished writing, give your story a title.

_____

_____

_____

_____

_____

_____

_____

_____

_____

_____

_____

_____

Answer Key

Page 5	1a	(3) Marty's trouble at school began when he chose the wrong seat.
	b	(3) Trouble for Marty
	2a	(3) a baby brother who cries because of a loose tooth.
	b	(1) The Loose Tooth
Page 6	1a	(1) a lost pencil found by its owner.
	b	(2) The Missing Pencil
	2a	(2) an injured hand
	b	(1) The Great Tetherball Injury
Page 7	1a	(3) a raccoon who washes his food before he eats it.
	b	(3) Getting Ready to Eat
	2a	(3) One beaver will warn other beavers of possible danger.
	b	(1) The Frightening Noise
Page 8	1	(3) Dolphins can talk by making sounds.
	2	(3) Hyenas make laugh-like sounds.
Page 9	a	(1) what porcupine quills look like and how they are used.
	b	(3) Porcupine Quills
Page 10	a	(1) 3, (2) 1, (3) 2, (4) 1, (5) 3, (6) 1, (7) 3, (8) 2, (9) 3, (10) 1
	b	(2) A Holiday Present for a Friend
Page 11	a	(1) 2, (2) 1, (3) 3, (4) 3, (5) 2, (6) 2, (7) 1, (8) 2, (9) 3, (10) 3
	b	(3) Flying Alone
Page 12	1a	Hitting your funny bone is not really funny.
	b	(3) Your Funny Bone
	2a	The kangaroo rat never drinks water.
	b	(3) The Kangaroo Rat
Page 13	1a	The groundhog is supposed to be able to predict the weather.
	b	(3) How Groundhogs Predict the Weather
	2a	Most of your dreams are based on things that have happened to you in your life.
	b	(1) Dreams
Page 14	1a	Mammals are one type of animal that scientists classify.
	b	To be mammals, animals must share certain characteristics.
	c	There are many different kinds of mammals.
	2a	Forty to eighty thousand bees live together in a beehive.
	b	All the bees in the hive have jobs.
Page 15	1a	Giraffes are the tallest animals in the world.
	b	Giraffes are vegetarians.
	c	Giraffes are gregarious.
	2a	Someone cut in front of me in line.
	b	Before recess, as I lined up to go outside, someone else cut in front of me.
	c	At lunchtime, another person took cuts.
	d	Today my problem was solved.
Page 16	1c	The puffer has a simple way of protecting itself.
	2b	The panda lives in bamboo jungles.
	3c	Snakes slither along flicking their tongues in and out.
	4a	A rhino's horn is not a real horn.
Page 17	1c	An elephant's trunk has many uses.
	2a	The polar bear is well suited to live in the snow.
	3b	The strangest thing about a seahorse is the way it raises its young.
	4a	The hedgehog has a unique way of protecting itself.
Page 18	1c	The mole is well suited for living underground.
	2a	A baby hippo is born underwater.
	3b	An elephant looks like it has enough skin to keep it warm or cool, but it doesn't.
	4b	The koala stays in trees most of the time.

Page 30   1a   The Kangaroo has a useful tail.

           b   (1) How far can a kangaroo jump?

               (2) How does the kangaroo use its tail when it leaps?

               (3) How does the kangaroo use its tail when it lands?

               (4) How does the kangaroo use its tail when it sits?

           c   Answers will vary.

           2a   The shrew is one of the hungriest animals in the world.

           b   (1) What is the name of one of the hungriest animals in the world?

               (2) How small is a shrew?

               (3) How does the shrew spend its waking hours?

               (4) How much food does the shrew eat?

           c   Answers will vary.

Page 31   1   Some black honey ants from South America are always filled with food.

           2a   Where do these black honey ants live?

           b   What are some of these black honey ants filled with?

           c   How large do their stomachs become?

           d   What do these ants do when food becomes scarce?

           e   What unusual treat do people who live in South America sometimes eat?

           3   Answers will vary.

Page 32   The dialogue should be rewritten in the same order. Check to see that the first word of each numbered paragraph has been indented.

Page 33   The dialogue should be rewritten in the same order. Check to see that a new paragraph has been begun each time a different speaker begins speaking and that the first word of each new paragraph has been indented.

Page 34   The story should be rewritten in the same order on a separate sheet of paper. Check to see that a new paragraph has been begun each time the dialogue moves from one speaker to another or the story moves from dialogue to narrative or narrative to dialogue. The words or phrases below each begin a new paragraph. The rewritten story should contain nineteen paragraphs.

Tom and Steve sat . . . .

Will you *please* give me . . .?"

"I only have one piece . . . ."

Mrs. Butterfield . . . .

"How can *I* get *you* . . ."

"It's almost time for lunch. . . ."

Steve blew on his fist . . . .

Tom laughed quietly . . . .

Steve shook his head and said , . . .

As the boys continued to talk, . . .

"These look easy," said Steve. . . .

Reluctantly, Tom nodded and handed Steve . . . .

"This gum is great!"

Just as he blew the first bubble, . . .

Steve ducked behind his open math book, . . .

"All right, boys and girls, . . ."

Steve felt his heart beating . . . .

"Guess what," said Tom.

For a moment, Steve stared at Tom . . . .

Pages 35-45   Students are asked to write one-paragraph, two-paragraph, and then three-paragraph stories inspired by pictures on these pages. Reponses will, of course, vary. Check to see that (1) each paragraph has a topic sentence, (2) the first word in each paragraph has been indented, (3) the sentences in each paragraph are in logical order, (4) the paragraphs in each story are in logical order, and (5) each story has been given a title.